Drawing and Learning About Monsters

Using Shapes and Lines

written and illustrated by
Amy Bailey Muehlenhardt

Thanks to our advisers for their expertise, research, and advice:

Linda Frichtel, Design Adjunct Faculty, MCAD
Minneapolis, Minnesota

Susan Kesselring, M.A., Literacy Educator
Rosemount–Apple Valley–Eagan (Minnesota) School District

PICTURE WINDOW BOOKS
Minneapolis, Minnesota

Amy Bailey Muehlenhardt
grew up in Fergus Falls, Minnesota,
and attended Minnesota State
University in Moorhead. She holds
a Bachelor of Science degree in
Graphic Design and Art Education.
Before coming to Picture Window
Books, Amy was an elementary art
teacher. She always impressed upon
her students that "everyone is an artist."
Amy lives in Mankato, Minnesota,
with her husband, Brad, and
daughter, Elise.

For Elise Lauren, my new smile.
ABM

Editorial Director: Carol Jones
Managing Editor: Catherine Neitge
Creative Director: Keith Griffin
Editor: Jill Kalz
Editorial Adviser: Bob Temple
Story Consultant: Terry Flaherty
Designer: Jaime Martens
Page Production: Picture Window Books
The illustrations in this book were created with pencil
and colored pencil.

Picture Window Books
5115 Excelsior Boulevard
Suite 232
Minneapolis, MN 55416
1-877-845-8392
www.picturewindowbooks.com

Printed in the United States of America.

Library of Congress Cataloging-in-Publication Data
Muehlenhardt, Amy Bailey, 1974–
Drawing and learning about monsters / written and illustrated by
Amy Bailey Muehlenhardt.
p. cm. — (Sketch it!)
Includes bibliographical references and index.
ISBN 1-4048-1195-8 (hardcover)
1. Monsters in art—Juvenile literature. 2. Drawing—Technique—
Juvenile literature. I. Title: Monsters. II. Title.
NC825.M6M84 2005
741.2—dc22   2005007178

Table of Contents

Everyone Is an Artist
There is no right or wrong way to draw!

With a little patience and some practice, anyone can learn to draw. Did you know every picture begins as a simple shape? If you can draw shapes, you can draw anything.

The Basics of Drawing

line—a long mark made by a pen, a pencil, or another tool

guideline—a line used to help you draw; the guideline will be erased when your drawing is almost complete

shade—to color in with your pencil

value—the lightness or darkness of an object

shape—the form or outline of an object or figure

diagonal—a shape or line that leans to the side

Before you begin, you will need

a pencil,
an eraser,
lots of paper!

Four Tips for Drawing

1. Draw very lightly.
Try drawing light, medium, and dark lines. The softer you press, the lighter the lines will be.

2. Draw your shapes.
When you are finished drawing, connect your shapes with a sketch line.

3. Add details.
Details are small things that make a good picture even better.

4. Color your art.
Use your colored pencils, crayons, or markers to create backgrounds.

Let's get started!

Simple shapes help you draw.

Practice drawing these shapes before you begin.

 **circle**
A circle is round like a ball.

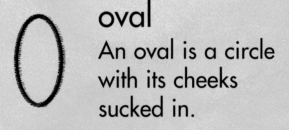 **oval**
An oval is a circle with its cheeks sucked in.

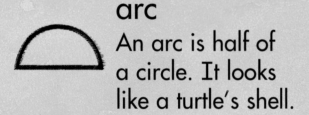 **arc**
An arc is half of a circle. It looks like a turtle's shell.

 **square**
A square has four equal sides and four corners.

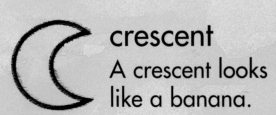 **crescent**
A crescent looks like a banana.

 **triangle**
A triangle has three sides and three corners.

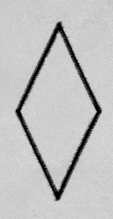 **diamond**
A diamond is two triangles put together.

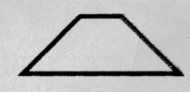 **trapezoid**
A trapezoid has four sides and four corners. Two of its sides are different lengths.

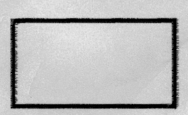 **rectangle**
A rectangle has two long sides, two short sides, and four corners.

You will also use lines when drawing.

Practice drawing these lines.

| vertical
A vertical line stands tall like a tree.

 zigzag
A zigzag line is sharp and pointy.

___ horizontal
A horizontal line lies down and takes a nap.

 wavy
A wavy line moves up and down like a roller coaster.

\ diagonal
A diagonal line leans to the side.

Remember to practice drawing.

While using this book, you may want to stop drawing at step five or six. That's great! Everyone is at a different drawing level.

 dizzy
A dizzy line spins around and around.

Don't worry if your picture isn't perfect. The important thing is to have fun.

Be creative!

Sea Serpent

The sea serpent lives within the depths of large lakes and oceans. With its scaly skin, wing-like flippers, and snake-like tail, the sea serpent looks like a huge underwater dragon.

Step 1

Draw two triangles for the snout. Add two wavy lines for the body.

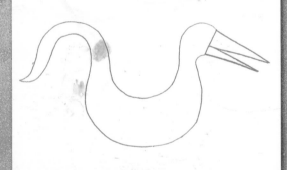

Step 2

Draw two arcs for the eyes and two arcs for the flippers.

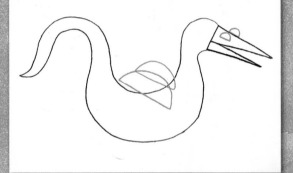

Step 3

Draw one zigzag line for the teeth. Add another zigzag line on the head and neck for the spikes.

Step 4

Draw wavy lines for the scales. Add small circles for the pupils.

Step 5

Define the monster with a sketch line. Define the flipper with a zigzag line.

Step 6

Erase the extra lines. Add details such as scales on the flippers.

Step 7

Color your monster and add a background.

Cyclops

A cyclops is easy to spot. A cyclops is a giant with just one eye—right in the middle of his forehead. He usually lives in caves and feeds on animals and people.

Step 1

Draw an arc for the head. Draw a rectangle for the body.

Step 2

Draw a rectangle for the legs. Add two ovals for the feet. Draw three circles for the eye.

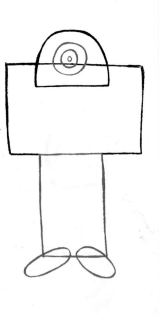

Step 3

Draw two vertical lines for the arms and one for the legs. Add 10 ovals for the fingers and 10 for the toes.

Step 4

Draw two crescents for the ears and one for the mouth.

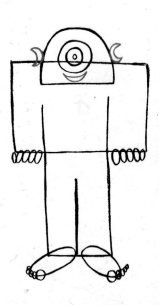

Step 5

Define the monster with a sketch line. Define the pants with two zigzag lines.

Step 6

Erase the extra lines. Add details such as hair, eyelashes, and teeth.

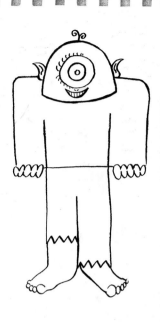

Step 7

Color your monster and add a background.

Bogeyman

The bogeyman sometimes hides in the bedrooms of naughty kids. He is always changing shape. Sometimes he has horns, fangs, or a long, spiky tail.

Step 1

Draw a trapezoid for the body and a triangle for the head. Add two circles for the eyes.

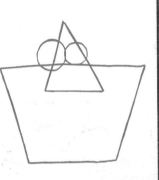

Step 2

Draw a rectangle for the legs and a circle for the stomach. Define the legs with a vertical line. Add two small circles for the pupils.

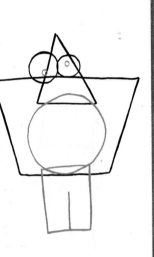

Step 3

Draw two ovals for the feet. Add eight ovals for the fingers. Add eight ovals for the toes.

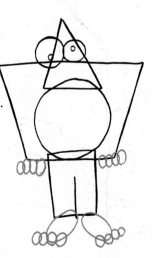

Step 4

Draw two crescents for the horns. Draw a triangle for the mouth. Add an oval for the nose.

Step 5

Define the monster with a zigzag sketch line.

Step 6

Erase the extra lines. Add details such as body hair and fangs.

Step 7

Color your monster and add a background.

Zombie

Zombies are the walking dead. After sunset, they rise out of their graves. Their tattered clothes cling to their gray, lifeless bodies. They usually walk in groups, stiffly and slowly, like robots.

Step 1

Draw two circles for the head. Draw an arc for the shoulders.

Step 2

Draw two arcs for the hands. Draw a square for the body. Add three rectangles for the legs.

Step 3

Draw two ovals for the feet. Draw 10 ovals for the fingers. Add 10 circles for the toes.

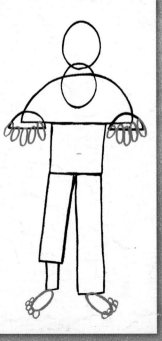

Step 4

Draw two ovals for the eyes. Draw two ovals and a triangle for the mouth. Add two arcs for the ears.

Step 5

Define the monster with a sketch line. Define the pants with two zigzag lines. Add two curved lines for the arms.

Step 6

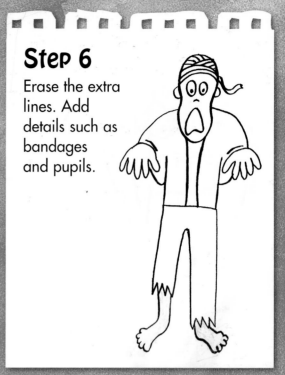

Erase the extra lines. Add details such as bandages and pupils.

Step 7

Color your monster and add a background.

Werewolf

The werewolf seems like a normal person by day. But when a full moon rises, fur starts growing all over his face and body. Sharp fangs jut out from behind his lips, and his howl fills the night air.

Step 1

Draw an oval for the head. Draw an arc for the shoulders. Add a square for the body.

Step 2

Draw four rectangles for the legs. Add two ovals for the feet. Draw two arcs for the hands.

Step 3

Draw eight triangles for the claws. Draw two circles and a triangle for the snout. Add two ovals for the eyes. Draw a square for the mouth.

Step 4

Draw two crescents for the ears. Draw a triangle for the nose. Add two arcs for the eyebrows.

16

Step 5

Define the monster with a sketch line. Draw zigzag lines for the hair and the ripped pants.

Step 6

Erase the extra lines. Add details such as whiskers and the insides of the ears.

Step 7

Color your monster and add a background.

Vampire

The sun sets, and the vampire rises from his coffin. Vampires have long fangs and wear black capes. They lurk in the shadows, looking for a neck to bite. Some vampires can turn themselves into bats or wolves.

Step 1

Draw one oval for the head and one for the body. Add six rectangles for the arms and legs. Add two ovals for the eyes.

Step 2

Draw two arcs for the hands. Draw two ovals for the feet. Draw two vertical lines for the neck. Add a horizontal line for the mouth.

Step 3

Draw two triangles and a circle for the bow tie. Add two zigzag lines for the claws. Add two crescents for the ears.

Step 4

Draw curved lines for the nose and the hair. Add two arcs for the eyebrows. Draw two triangles for the fangs.

Step 5

Draw a wavy line for the wings. Add a trapezoid for the cape. Add a zigzag line for the body hair. Define the monster with a sketch line.

Step 6

Erase the extra lines. Add details such as hair and wing folds.

Step 7

Color your monster and add a background.

Alien

People come in all shapes, sizes, and colors—so do aliens! Aliens are beings from places beyond our planet. This alien has a thin body with a human shape, but its large eyes and huge, egg-shaped head make it stand out.

Step 1

Draw an oval for the head. Draw one rectangle for the neck and one for the body.

Step 2

Draw four rectangles for the arms. Add two ovals and a triangle for each hand. Draw two ovals for the eyes.

Step 3

Draw two arcs for the legs. Draw two ovals for the feet. Add a horizontal line for the mouth.

Step 4

Draw two trapezoids for the mouth. Add four triangles for the claws. Draw a triangle for the shirt neckline.

Step 5
Define the monster with a sketch line.

Step 6
Erase the extra lines. Add details such as teeth. Draw curved lines to define the eyes.

Step 7
Color your monster and add a background.

Swamp Monster

A dark, hunchbacked figure rises out of the swamp. Seaweed hangs from its head and arms. Muddy water drips from its hairy body. The swamp monster is a quiet creature that leaves no trace, except for its huge footprints.

Step 1
Draw one oval for the body and one for the head.

Step 2
Draw four ovals for the arms. Add two circles for the hands.

Step 3
Draw five ovals for the legs.

Step 4
Draw 14 triangles for the claws. Add two ovals for the eyes. Draw two short lines for the nose.

Step 5

Draw two dots inside the eyes for the pupils. Add two triangles for the teeth. Define the monster with a sketch line.

Step 6

Erase the extra lines. Add details such as wet seaweed.

Step 7

Color your monster and add a background.

At the Library

Barr, Steve. *1-2-3 Draw Cartoon Monsters: A Step-by-Step Guide.* Cincinnati, Ohio: North Light Books, 2004.

Kistler, Mark. *Dare to Draw in 3-D: Monster Mania.* New York: Scholastic, 2002.

McLaughlin, Frank. *How to Draw Monsters for Comics.* Los Angeles: Renaissance Books, 2001.

Reinagle, Damon J. *Draw Monsters: A Step-by-Step Guide.* Columbus, N.C.: Peel Productions, 2005.

On the Web

FactHound

FactHound offers a safe, fun way to find Web sites related to this book.

All of the sites on FactHound have been researched by our staff.

http://www.facthound.com

1. Visit the FactHound home page.
2. Enter a search word related to this book, or type in this special code: 1404811958.
3. Click on the FETCH IT button.

Your trusty FactHound will fetch the best sites for you!

Look for all the books in the Sketch It! series:
Drawing and Learning About ...

Bugs	Faces	Monsters
Cars	Fashion	Monster Trucks
Cats	Fish	
Dinosaurs	Horses	
Dogs	Jungle Animals	

24